Unlocking the BODY'S CODE: Reclaiming Your Health and Happiness fromTrauma

Jamie C. Summer

Table of Contents

INTRODUCTION

- **THE HIDDEN LANGUAGE OF THE BODY**

Our body has a secret language, an approach to recounting the narrative of our lives that goes beyond anything describable. It talks through your sentiments, hurts, and sensations. This book is tied in with understanding that secret language, how your body recalls your encounters, both great and awful, and what it means for your wellbeing and joy.Imagine your body as a narrator, sharing the stories of your past through actual sensations. Very much like learning another dialect, we'll investigate how to translate these signs. By understanding this language, you can mend past difficulties, fabricate flexibility, and assume responsibility for your prosperity.In the sections ahead, we'll reveal the mysteries of this secret language, giving you the apparatus to change your life by understanding and working with your body's messages.

CHAPTER 1: UNDERSTANDING TRAUMA

- **WHAT IS TRAUMA?**

Trauma is any kind of upsetting occasion or experience that can affect an individual's capacity to adapt and work. Injury can result in close to home, physical, and mental mischief. Many individuals will encounter a horrendous mishap of some sort — from the unforeseen demise of

a friend or family member to an engine vehicle mishap — eventually in the course of their life. Nonetheless, not all individuals will foster post horrendous pressure issues after a horrible mishap. Despite the fact that somebody probably won't foster PTSD, they might in any case encounter PTSD-like side effects following a horrendous mishap.

Tyes

Trauma comes in many shapes and structures, however a few normal situations are for the most part thought to be horrendous. Kinds of horrendous mishaps that an individual might insight eventually in life include:

Misuse

Attack

Auto Crash

Passing of a friend or family member

Separate

Family or parental deserting

Detainment

Employment cutback

Catastrophic events

Actual trauma

Assault

Difficult ailment

Psychological oppression

Viciousness

Seeing a wrongdoing, mishap, or passing

Trauma frequently can be categorized as one of three unique classes. few

Trauma , like mishaps or catastrophic events, are one-time occasions that are

restricted in term and extension. Different traumas are enduring and continuous,

like adapting to a persistent disease or managing rehashed homegrown

maltreatment. There are likewise kinds of trauma that are frequently disregarded,

For example, trauma that happens during labor or medical procedure.

Side effects

All in all, what is a "typical" side effect versus an "unusual" side effect of

trauma.This is hard to reply as everybody's reaction to a horrible mishap is

unique.There are, in any case, a few normal side effects that might be supposed to

happen after a horrendous mishap. Coming up next are a few normal responses to trauma.Meddlesome contemplations and recollections: After a horrendous mishap, encountering a few nosy considerations and recollections of the horrible accident is normal. This is particularly liable to happen when you experience something (for instance, an individual, spot, or picture) that helps you to remember the horrible mishap.

Hypervigilance: It is likewise exceptionally normal to feel more wary and mindful of your environmental elements after a horrendous mishap. This is an exceptionally defensive side effect, as your body is endeavoring to guard you by making you more mindful of expected wellsprings of danger and risk. This normal security components will be more delicate following a horrendous mishap.

Hyperarousal: Similarly as you are probably going to be more wary, you are

likewise liable to feel more keyed up and nervous following a horrible mishap.

This is again essential for your body's regular insurance framework. Dread and

tension let us know that there is some sort of risk present, and every one of the

substantial vibes that accompany dread and nervousness are basically intended to

assist us with answering that risk. They are setting us up to escape, freeze, or

battle. Following a horrendous mishap, your body's caution framework will be

more delicate trying to shield you from future horrible mishaps.

Feeling risky: After a horrendous mishap, our suppositions about the world being free from even a hint of harm are justifiably broken. Thus, individuals might feel

like any circumstance or spot is possibly hazardous. Spots or circumstances you

once had a solid sense of safety and may now feel undermining and uneasiness

inciting. This is particularly liable to happen in circumstances or spots that help

you remember your horrible accident."Ordinary" Trauma Reaction versus

PTSD.As you read through certain side effects that ordinarily happen following a

horrendous mishap, you will see that most are likewise side effects of PTSD. It is

critical to recall that having these side effects doesn't mean you have PTSD. Albeit

the side effects underneath can be upsetting, they are in many cases significantly

less extreme and extraordinary than the side effects tracked down in PTSD. PTSD
can't be analyzed until no less than 30 days following a horrendous mishap in light
of the fact that numerous PTSD-like side effects are essential for your body's
regular reaction to a horrendous accident, and for some individuals, these side
effects will continuously decrease over the long run.

Side effects to Look For

The side effects introduced underneath can be an indication that you might be in
danger of creating PTSD.3 They might cause the normal injury side effects
recorded above to turn out to be more terrible, ultimately prompting PTSD. In this
manner, it is vital to know about the accompanying side effects:

Loss of interest: It means a lot to watch out for a deficiency of interest in exercises that you used to once appreciate, as well as sensations of being disengaged from others. This side effect can be an indication that you are in danger of becoming discouraged. This side effect may likewise make you disconnect yourself from others, including significant wellsprings of social help.

Evasion: After a horrendous mishap, it is exceptionally considered normal to keep away from specific circumstances, exercises, or individuals. In any case, you should focus on avoiding ways of behaving. Evasion typically prompts more evasion, as it supports the conviction that the world is certainly not a protected

spot. This evasion can then prompt a deteriorating of side effects and, at last,
PTSD.

Unfortunate adapting ways of behaving: Similarly as aversion of exercises,
circumstances, or individuals can be dangerous, so can the evasion of
considerations and sentiments. The side effects individuals experience after a
Horrendous mishap can be very troublesome. Subsequently, individuals might
depend on undesirable survival techniques (for instance, utilizing substances) as an
approach to staying away from these side effects. Evasion is just a transient
arrangement, and over the long haul, it can make your sentiments and
considerations become more extraordinary.

Diagnosis

In the event that you are having side effects of injury, you might be determined to
have a condition like PTSD. Nonetheless, it is essential to recall that not all
horrendous encounters will prompt a finding of a trauma related condition. At the
point when you converse with your PCP or psychological wellness proficient, they
will pose inquiries about the side effects you are encountering and the way in
which quite a while in the past the injury happened.In the event that you are as yet
encountering side effects for quite a while after the experience and these side
effects essentially affect your everyday living, your PCP will verify whether you
meet the symptomatic models for an injury or stressor-related jumble or

conceivably a change problem, contingent upon the specific idea of your side
effects.

Treatment

In the event that you have encountered injury, it might very well be useful to
converse with a specialist. Take a stab at asking your primary care physician or a
friend or family member for a proposal. A few sites give free ventures to assist you
with finding proper emotional well-being suppliers in your space accessible
through the U.S. Branch of Veterans Undertakings. A specialist can offer help, as
as well as assisting you with better comprehension of the side effects you are
experiencing.

Treatment will rely upon the side effects you are encountering because of the trauma. It might include psychotherapy, drugs, taking care of oneself, or a blend of

these methodologies. Medicines frequently center around assisting individuals with

incorporating their profound reaction to the injury as well as tending to any

subsequent psychological well-being conditions like uneasiness, despondency, or

PTSD.

What Is Basic Episode Stress Interviewing?

Psychotherapy

Treatment might include the utilization of mental conduct treatment (CBT) to assist

individuals with assessing considerations and sentiments connected with injury and

Supplant negative reasoning with additional practical contemplations. Eye

development desensitization and going back over (EMDR) is one more methodology that uses components of CBT joined with eye or body developments.

Prescriptions

On the off chance that you have been determined to have PTSD because of trauma,

a few meds may likewise be useful as a piece of your treatment. These drugs might include: Antidepressants, including serotonin reuptake inhibitors (SSRIs) like Paxil (paroxetine) and Zoloft (sertraline), the two of which have been endorsed by the

FDA for the treatment of PTSD Hostile to uneasiness drugs, for example, benzodiazepines including Valium

(diazepam) and Ativan (lorazepam)

How is PTSD treated ?

Adapting

In the wake of encountering a horrible mishap, it is vital to establish solid survival techniques, like utilizing social help and limiting unfortunate methods for dealing

with especially difficult times, like evasion through liquor or drugs.

A things that you can do to assist cycle and adapt to trauma are:

Approve your sentiments.

 You don't need to drive yourself to converse with

others about how you feel; in any case, you mustn't attempt to drive away your

sentiments. Find a care group where you can converse with others who have gone

through comparative encounters.Give yourself an opportunity to manage what you are feeling. Try not to anticipate that these sentiments should disappear for the time

being. Meanwhile, make an effort not to stress about yourself.

Deal with your body

Eat ordinary nutritious feasts, attempt to get sufficient rest, and participate in active work routinely.

Invest energy with loved ones. Despite the fact that you could want to be separated from everyone else, secluding yourself can make it more challenging to manage the impacts of trauma. Permit yourself to rest on individuals who care about and support you.It might likewise be useful to lay out a daily practice or timetable.

Horrible mishaps can significantly disturb an individual's life. They might cause an individuals feel that their life is wild and eccentric. A normal set timetable can assist with carrying a request and consistency to your life.Albeit adhering to a routine won't remove uneasiness connected with the horrible mishap, it might

assist with different wellsprings of nervousness in your life. In setting a timetable,

you should set to the side time zeroed in on taking care of oneself exercises and

guard against involving your timetable as an approach to just keep occupied (for

instance, hurling yourself entirely into your work) so you lack opportunity and

willpower to ponder the horrendous mishap.

- **IMPACT OF TRAUMA**

The Effect of trauma: Inconspicuous Injuries and Mending Ways

Trauma is a word weighed down with importance, meaning the actual wounds it

might invoke as well as the covered up, persevering through injuries scratched into

the actual texture of one's being.
The effect of trauma rises above
the second it
happens, broadening its venture
into each aspect of a singular's
life, shaping their
contemplations, feelings, and
activities. A quiet yet powerful
power makes a
permanent imprint. Trauma can
appear in endless structures: the
tragic
pulverization of a cataclysmic
event, the eerie recollections of
battle, the scars left
by actual maltreatment, or the
tenacious profound injuries from
youth disregard. Its
belongings might be pretty much
as individual as individuals who
experience it,
yet they share consistent ideas,
winding around an embroidery of
torment, strength,
and trust.

Profound and Mental Scars

At the core of injury's effects are the close to home and mental scars. They come in

many structures, from the tension that keeps an individual never-endingly nervous

to the profundities of misery that drive them into a persevering pit. Trauma can

raise bad dreams and flashbacks that transport people back to the excruciating

minutes, over and over. These profound scars can prompt Post-Horrendous

Pressure Issue

(PTSD), a condition portrayed by incapacitating side effects that obstruct day to

day existence.

Survival techniques and Conduct Changes

The impacts of trauma frequently reach out into one's way of behaving. While

trying to safeguard themselves from additional damage, people might foster hypervigilance, continually checking their environmental factors for indications of

risk. This can prompt aversion, as they look to reduce most, if not all, connection

with whatever might set off their trauma. Disassociation, a strategy for dealing

with especially difficult times that disconnects them from the truth, is another

normal reaction. Trust issues may likewise emerge, as past double-crossings cast

shadows on future connections.

Inner Strife

Trauma much of the time brings forth a whirlwind of feelings. Culpability and

disgrace can be overpowering, particularly assuming that the trauma is related with

sensations of weakness or weakness. Melancholy for the deficiency of honesty or well being might endure for quite a long time. The deficiency of command over

one's own life can be anguishing, causing a feeling of weakness that pervades each

part of presence.

Disengagement and Self-Uncertainty

Trauma can significantly disengage. The individuals who have experienced may

feel removed from other people who can't grasp the profundities of their

aggravation.They might pull out from social associations and become

progressively secluded. Self-question is another slippery buddy, frequently

murmuring that they are some way or another to blame for their trauma, that they

ought to have done something contrastingly to forestall it.While the effect of trauma is irrefutable and unavoidable, there is trust. Mending isn't just imaginable, however achievable. The excursion toward recuperation includes perceiving the

impacts of trauma, looking for help from experts, and, in particular, tracking down

the internal solidarity to modify one's life. The scars might remain, however they

need not direct one's future. Understanding the effect of trauma is the initial step on a way towards recuperating

and flexibility. It is a demonstration of the human soul that people can make due as

well as flourish subsequent to encountering trauma. With the right help, a

sustaining climate, and the assurance to face the past, individuals can rise out of the

shadow of, areas of strength for trauma strong, prepared to embrace life once

- **HOW TRAUMA AFFECTS YOUR BODY**

At the point when somebody encounters trauma, it's typical for them to have actual sensations like cerebral pains, exhaustion, annoyed stomach, and muscle pressure. Individuals may likewise encounter melancholy and nervousness, in addition to long haul actual side effects related to these issues.

These side effects include:

- Diminished torment resistance

-

- Dozing issues

-

- Dyspepsia
  Muscle hurts

- Dyspepsia and gastrointestinal issues

-

- Windedness

-

- Weight reduction

-

- Sadly, over the long haul, profound injury can prompt long haul medical

-

- issues. As indicated by research, horrendous

mishaps can set off physical

-
- and close to home responses that can make individuals more inclined to
-
- creating difficult circumstances, including diabetes, stroke, cardiovascular
-
- failure, corpulence, and diseases
-
-
-
-
-
-
-
-
-
-
-
-
-
-
-
-
-
-

CHAPTER II: DECODING THE BODY MESSAGES

THE MIND BODY CONNECTION

You may currently know all about phrases that portray the psyche body

association in everyday life, for example, something being a "major irritation",

making your "blood bubble", having a "premonition" or being "heart-broken".

These models all portray the way
that the brain can influence the
body. In this flier,
when we discuss the 'mind' we
mean the assortment of
contemplations, sentiments,
convictions, mentalities,
recollections, previous
encounters, and character that
make up an individual's interior
world. Is everything in my mind?
It is essential to
call attention to that in this
pamphlet we are not
recommending your actual side
effects are a figment of your
imagination. The truth of your
actual side effects isn't
in uncertainty when we discuss
the brain and body being
connected. It is vital to
make this reasonable on the
grounds that we know that a few
patients, at some
time, have felt that their
challenges were excused by
others, including medical
services experts, as "a figment of
their imagination". How can it
function? The
cerebrum and the body are
continually sending messages to
one another. These

messages advise the mind and body to make changes and acclimations to the manner in which they are working. For instance, on the off chance that your eyes told your mind a vehicle was going towards you at speed, it would send an extremely quick message to the body to step back out of danger. Also, assuming your stomach was unfilled and your body required fuel, your cerebrum would pay attention to that message and send you looking for food. In this way, the psyche and the body is in consistent correspondence to keep you solid.

Battle Flight System

An illustration of this cozy connection between the brain and body is the 'Battle Flight' system. This alert framework was created to guard us from risk, similar to the danger of hunters, for instance. It is set off when you feel undermined, and it

causes your body to prepare for a
battle or for taking off (e.g., by
making your
heart beat quicker and your
muscles worry). These actual
side effects are the
consequence of the arrival of
stress chemicals in the body, like
cortisol and
adrenaline. This functioned
admirably when there were
hunters around. Tragically,
it is less useful for advanced
dangers. Things like cash stresses
or fears over the
future can set off this 'survival'
reaction, regardless of whether it
isn't so useful for
taking care of the issue. Constant
versus intense pressure Attempt
to eat an even
eating routine spread across the
day. This might assist your body
with fending off
contaminations and When the
'Battle Flight' instrument is
enacted once in a while,
The body can adapt and
recuperate well after the flood of
pressure chemicals. This
is in some cases called 'intense
pressure and we are intended to
manage this. 2

Notwithstanding, when the 'Battle Flight' instrument is enacted frequently, the body has less opportunity to recuperate before the following distressing occasion completely. This is called 'ongoing pressure' and we are less very much adjusted to this sort of pressure.

The strong job of contemplations

"For there isn't anything either positive or negative, however thinking works everything out." Despite the fact that we are not confronted with saber-toothed tigers consistently, life presents heaps of circumstances that can be seen as undermining and triggering this pressure reaction. Our contemplations and decisions about circumstances play a vital part in deciding if this pressure reaction is set off or not. For instance, in the event that you ran for the transport and promptly a while later had awkward side effects like a beating heart and perspiring,

you could have the thought,
"Golly, I'm not generally so fit as
I used to be" and
proceed with your excursion as
expected with no extraordinary
change by the way
you feel. Notwithstanding, on the
off chance that you had a family
background
Of coronary failures and had a
new determination of
hypertension yourself, you
would rather have the idea, "I'm
having a respiratory failure" feel
extremely
terrified, and called an
emergency vehicle. This model
shows that a similar
encounter, deciphered in an
unexpected way, can bring about
totally different
sentiments and decisions.
The brain body connects and
your wellbeing A portion of the
body's frameworks
are more impacted by the psyche
body interface than others. You
might perceive
some recorded beneath. Stomach
related Framework Changes It is
normal to

encounter an irritated stomach
(e.g., sickness, the runs, swelling,
or agony) during
seasons of pressure. There are
bunches of nerve associations
between the cerebrum
and the stomach. The stomach is
sometimes called the 'Little
Mind',consequently.The vast
majority have encountered this
kind of psyche body
association at some time. For
instance, perhaps you have had a
stirring stomach
when you were fearing
something or required the latrine
critically prior to
something significant like a
meeting. It is notable that the
stomach is impacted by
the 'battle flight' response. It has
even been proposed that having
an unfilled
bladder and gut might have
assisted our progenitors with
escaping from hunters.
Essentially, individuals who have
a finding of Touchy Gut
Condition (IBS) say
their side effects are impacted by
pressure.
Skin Conditions

Individuals with skin conditions,
including dermatitis or psoriasis,
notice that
during distressing periods their
side effects can turn out to be
more regrettable and
answer less well to traditional
medicines. These eruptions can
thus increase stress
making an endless loop. For
instance, individuals might stress
over their skin
appearance and the way that
others will see them or be
irritated by awkward
tingling and the inclination to
scratch. These burdens can stack
up, now and again
disturbing the skin further or
halting it quieting down as fast.
Heart Side effects
Changes in the manner the heart
works are normal in unpleasant
or energizing
conditions. For instance, stress or
fervor can make the heart beat
quicker and raise
the pulse. This is important for
the 'Battle Flight' reaction and
assists you with
preparing to take off or battle the
danger. Albeit these heart side
effects can be

upsetting they are not perilous
and consistently die down
without help from anyone
else after some time without
causing you any damage. These
typical shifts in
perspective rate and circulatory
strain because of stress can be
disturbing for
individuals regardless of heart
conditions. Stressing that your
side effects might be
an indication of something
serious can be very startling.
These concerns, and the
Pressure and uneasiness that go
with them, can build these 'Battle
Flight '- related
heart side effects, making an
endless loop. Breathing
Hardships Windedness is a
disagreeable side effects that the
vast majority have encountered.
For instance, you
might be winded in the wake of
running for the transport,
especially in the event
that you are not used to running.
Windedness can likewise be
associated with
ailments like asthma or ongoing
obstructive respiratory illness.
This windedness

can be an extremely terrifying
encounter, especially in the
Evening if you dread something
horrendous could happen like
dropping or not
having the option to get your
next breath. These
considerations, and the
apprehension and nervousness
related with them, can welcome
additional actual
side effects, including more
windedness. These side effects
can cause it to appear
to be significantly almost certain
that something dreadful is going
to occur. For
certain individuals, this might
prompt a fit of anxiety. While
staying away from
circumstances that trigger
shortness of breath, for example
movement frequently
appears as though a sensible
arrangement, it is typically
pointless genuinely and
sincerely over the long haul.

Torment

Torment is a perplexing side
effect that can here and there be
hard to comprehend

and treat. This is on the grounds
that it is an extremely private and
emotional

experience. It shouldn't be visible
on an output or estimated by a
blood test.

Torment is both a physical and
close to home insight and is
impacted by the brain

and the body. For instance, the
experience of torment can be
impacted by pressure,

tension, and discouragement.
Some aggravation conditions,
similar to headache

and different migraines, can be
set off in certain people by
physical and profound

Pressure

Weakness

Weakness is another complex
actual side effect that, similar to
torment, is

impacted by physical and mental
elements. Generally, weakness
follows active

work, absence of rest, or
extensive stretches of
attentiveness. Weariness can
likewise be a side effect of
specific ailments as well as a
result of certain

prescriptions. Nonetheless, exhaustion can likewise be impacted by how we think and feel. For instance, weariness can prompt an inclination to be exhausted and languid, though a startling piece of uplifting news could provide you with an eruption of energy. Weakness can likewise be available as a feature of temperament issues like sorrow and nervousness. Individuals who experience medical conditions might battle with exhaustion which is a blend of physical and profound variables.

How would care and body influence one another?

Actual Elements The manner in which actual changes in the body happen because of our viewpoints, sentiments, and responses isn't completely perceived. Notwithstanding, beneath are a few potential components. Stress Chemicals and their Belongings The body's pressure chemicals, which incorporate adrenaline and

cortisol, are intended to have a
transient impact, giving us
enough actual energy
and solidarity to escape
hazardous circumstances. This
flood of 'Battle Flight'
chemicals can have impermanent
impacts, for example, a raised
pulse, perspiring,
shaking, windedness, and so on.
Notwithstanding, when these
chemicals are
delivered habitually, they are
remembered to affect the body,
influencing how it
functions overall. All this might
make it harder for the body to
keep its organs and
frameworks filling in as they
ought to, for instance. The
invulnerable framework
might be less successful when
stress chemicals are delivered
consistently, for
example ongoing pressure. This
might be on the grounds that the
body centers
around the errand it considers to
be generally significant, staying
away from the
danger, as opposed to utilizing
energy to identify
contaminations, for instance, and

monitor them. n Recuperating is dialed back. Like the safe framework, when the
the body accepts it is enduring an onslaught, it puts errands that are not promptly
fundamental, such as fixing harmed cells, as a second thought. While this is alright temporarily, in the long haul, it can create actual issues by dialing back
recuperation. n Processing, such as recuperating, is likewise placed as a second
thought during seasons of pressure, which can prompt stomach related distresses
like stomach torment, queasiness, clogging, looseness of the bowels, and bulging,
for instance. Mental Elements Figuring styles can influence how you feel
genuinely and actually. Some normal reasoning styles cause it to appear to be
probable that something terrible will occur. This can prompt inclination, stress, and
misery.

Thinking Styles

What you think — your 'thinking style' — can mean how you feel genuinely and actually. Some normal reasoning styles cause it to appear to be probable that something terrible will occur. This can cause you to feel stressed, miserable, or resentful, despite the fact that the idea isn't correct. You might perceive a portion of the models beneath. Thinking style What you might think when you feel restless.

Figuring out your condition

At the point when you have a medical condition, it is typical to attempt to figure it out by working out how it affects you and your life. The manner in which you feel about the issue and how you manage it might depend upon the responses to a few significant inquiries, for example,

What sort of issue am I confronting? Is it minor or serious?

What is my opinion about it? Am I stressed, focused, or down about it?

Might I at any point adapt to this issue, and what is my opinion about it? n Are the things I'm doing to attempt to adapt to working? Your responses will influence how you feel, both outwardly and inwardly. They will likewise influence what you feel ready to do it every day. In the long haul, they might try to influence how restricted you are by your condition. Consider these two models: Dave has been determined to have hypertension. Dave accepts this is an intense and hazardous conclusion since his dad kicked the bucket from a coronary episode. He has an exceptionally stressed outlook on it and questions whether he can adapt. He has attempted to care for himself by practicing as the specialist prompted, yet this appeared to exacerbate him, making him more stressed, so he halted. He battled to adhere to the extreme activity system he set for himself, so he feels remorseful and embarrassed too.

Brian likewise has hypertension. Brian realizes it isn't something he can overlook,
yet he accepts it is normal and treatable, so he isn't exceptionally stressed over it. He addressed his GP, who endorsed some drugs and offered him advice about his
eating routine and exercise. He goes out and works out, despite the fact that he
doesn't feel like it. Yet, in the event that he misses his exercise center meeting or
runs, he does whatever it takes not to whip himself about it and gets straight once
more into it the following day. These models show that your contemplations and
convictions about your condition and your adapting abilities are significant and can
influence how you deal with your side effects.

Assumptions

Our assumptions regarding what is going to happen can influence the sort of
involvement we have. For instance, studies have shown that individuals hoping to

feel torment report more
grounded torment when given an
innocuous electric shock
compared to those not expecting
torment given a similar shock.
This could imply
that anticipating that assessments
or methods should be difficult
and undesirable
and pondering the torment you
hope to feel could aggravate the
experience. Actual
Factors and Feeling Down
Believing down or discouraged
can affect your body.
Weariness, unfortunate rest,
changes in craving, and
expanded throbbing pain are
undeniably connected with
feeling down and discouraged. It
very well may be
challenging to distinguish these
actual side effects from different
side effects you
might have.

Nervousness

At the point when you are scared
or restless, you can likewise get
bunches of actual
side effects, for example, a
dashing heart, perspiring,
shaking, feeling unsteady,

and feeling wiped out. Although these side effects are not perilous, they are frequently undesirable, and you can wrongly think they are indications of a more difficult conditions.

Outrage

The progressions that occur in your body when you are furious are like those that happens when you are restless. Your heart might pulsate quicker, and you might begin to perspire and feel hot and tense. Others might see you as being very flushed and embarrassed. Your decisions and reactions The things you do A few things you really do will positively affect your body and psyche, like eating a decent eating regimen, working out, and having a decent rest schedule. Setting aside a few minutes for charming things like side interests, getting out, and meeting individuals can likewise help (see page nine). Different things, like smoking, utilizing medications, or drinking a lot of liquor, can meaningfully affect your physical and close-to-home prosperity, despite the fact that they appear to help temporarily.

 The things you don't do

Keeping away from things as a result of dread, feeling down, or actual uneasiness can make life simpler for the time being. This is on the grounds that you don't need to confront what you dread, conquer the inclination that you can't be irritated, or have more disagreeable actual side effects. Yet, in the long haul, this can be pointless. For instance, you can turn out to be more restless on the grounds that you can't be sure whether your apprehensions will work out as expected. It can imply that you continue to feel down or feel much more dreadful in light of the fact that you never have an opportunity to have a great time, delight, or pride. It can likewise make you sure that you can't have a full and dynamic existence without

terrible actual side effects, which may not be available, or furious, whether or not

the idea is valid or not. You might perceive a portion of the models on the

following page.

Thinking Styles

What you think — your 'thinking style' — can mean for how you feel genuinely

and actually. Some normal reasoning styles cause it to appear to be probable that something terrible will occur. This can cause you to feel stressed, miserable, or resentful, despite the fact that the idea isn't correct. You might perceive a portion of

the models beneath. Thinking style What you might think

- **UNRAVELING THE CODE OF TRAUMA**

One of the key parts of disentangling the code of trauma is recognizing the variety of awful encounters. Every individual's trauma is special and impacted by their singular history, science, and climate. This uniqueness can make injury testing to decipher and comprehend, as what significantly influences one individual may not influence one more similarly. Subsequently, the code of trauma is complex, requiring a diverse way to deal with unwinding its secrets. Neuroscience has given significant bits of knowledge into what injury means for the mind. At the point when an individual encounters trauma, the cerebrum pressure reaction framework becomes enacted, prompting the arrival of stress chemicals like cortisol. This elevated state can make a permanent imprint on the cerebrum, influencing memory, profound guidelines, and, surprisingly, the actual design of the organ. Understanding these neurological changes is a critical stage in unwinding the code of trauma,as it demystifies why people answer trauma in

unambiguous, once in a while
apparently peculiar, ways.
Additionally, the code of trauma
is well established in feelings and
recollections.
Horrendous mishaps are much of
the time engraved in striking,
nosy flashbacks,
bad dreams, or close to home
responses. These recollections
can be overpowering
to such an extent that they upset
day to day existence and
connections, catching
people previously. The test lies
in translating and handling these
horrendous
recollections, permitting the
individual to coordinate them
into their biography
without being overpowered by
them.
During the time spent
disentangling the code of trauma,
brain research assumes a
vital part. Remedial modalities
like mental social Treatment
(CBT) and eye
development desensitization and
going back over (EMDR) offer
instruments to

assist people with defying and reevaluating their awful encounters. By tending to the close to home and mental parts of trauma, these treatments enable survivors to recover command over their lives.

Social help is one more critical component in the code of injury. Confinement and an absence of understanding from loved ones can worsen the impacts of trauma. Building an organization of steady connections can give a feeling of safety and having a place, which is fundamental for recuperating. Moreover, society's acknowledgment and affirmation of injury as a genuine, crippling condition can assist with decreasing shame and make it simpler for survivors to look for help.

Disentangling the code of trauma is definitely not a straight cycle. A continuous excursion changes enormously from one individual to another. A few people might

track down comfort and mending
through treatment and backing,
while others
might go to inventive outlets like
craftsmanship or writing to
communicate their
encounters. By the way, the
consistent idea is the requirement
for self-empathy,
tolerance, and determination
even with the unpredictable and
frequently
languishing code of trauma.
Understanding and mending the
code of injury is a complex yet
fundamental
undertaking. It requires a diverse
methodology that thinks about
the interesting
idea of every individual's insight,
digs into the neurological and
mental parts of
trauma, and stresses the
significance of social help and
self-empathy. As we keep
on investigating the secrets of
trauma, we inch more like a
reality where the secret
traumas of the past are as of now
not difficult boundaries to a
satisfying and
significant life.

- **HOW MEMORIES SHAPES YOUR HEALTH**

What can influence our memory? To investigate this thought it's useful to initially ponder memory itself, and how it

tends to be impacted. Dissimilar to in Back to front, our recollections are not

glossy spheres that can be put away perfectly away, they are heaps of various and

particular memories, rambling all through our cerebrum. Our drawn out

recollections truly do to be sure have an actual presence in the mind, with

comparative recollections frequently bunching together. It's additionally commonly

acknowledged that feeling influences memory - now and again, it makes an

occasion more paramount, however it can make the contrary difference and lead to

cognitive decline.

Anguish, for instance, can crumble recollections. Studies have shown that those

encountering "convoluted
distress" (when sensations of
melancholy don't ease over
the long haul) can find it hard to
review recollections that don't
include the
cherished one who's passed,
trauma is frequently connected to
cognitive decline.
The person who knows nothing
about the trauma on a story level
and can adapt to
regular daily existence. There are
the pieces of the character that
hold the trauma
recollections. Parts that are
alarmed, ignorant that one is
currently protected. As far
as I might be concerned, these
parts are around constantly, yet
I'm frequently just
mindful of them on the off
chance that something triggers
me."
Dementia, and particularly
Alzheimer's sickness, are
different circumstances
related to cognitive decline. This
can be decimating to the
individual living with
the condition, and everyone
around them. The manner in
which recollections shift

and slip relies upon the
conclusion, and how advanced
the illness is.
"A few occasions, no matter
what our memory of them, can
score a profound line
in the book of our lives"
Then we have a mind trauma, a
memory cheat that comes
unannounced and
commonly follows a mishap
where the cerebrum has been
harmed. Once more, the
way this influences memory will
contrast from one individual to
another, for
certain individuals lose
recollections, while others can't
shape new ones.
How does cognitive decline
influence character?
As you might expect, there are
no obvious responses here, and
truly it will rely
upon the individual who's
accomplished the cognitive
decline
A few occasions, no matter what
our memory of them, can score a
profound line in
the book of our lives. For some
purposes, a supportive
methodology is to just turn

the page and push ahead.
"Continuously something is
being made - a task, piece of
craftsmanship, execution,
or lunch to anticipate, and
individuals are changed into
entertainers in times where
the personality is situated in the
present and what's in store."
 Our identity depends on our jobs
and how we connect with others.
"We are girls
and children, perhaps guardians
or kin, pet people, and
companions. These are
gigantic jobs and we could
improve to develop them! I
presently effectively search
for alternate ways that
personality can be created which
don't depend on memory,
yet rather on something that
associates us to the present time
and place. Whether
this includes making something,
or an approach to interfacing
with somebody."
Close by our jobs, our ethical
qualities can likewise hold
importance, with
research demonstrating that
ethical personality is of more
significance than

memory in saving a healthy identity in dementia.

"Our ethical qualities, including our sympathy, empathy, and our worthy frameworks, are somewhat protected in Alzheimer's sickness, and express more about us rather than our recollections."

What our identity is, then, at that point, can't be restricted to the recollections we hold. Certain encounters will most likely influence our personality, yet it isn't really the memory of these occasions that characterizes us, yet our response to them. Our personality is embroidery, with various strands twisting together to make us.

Adapting

On the off chance that you've encountered cognitive decline, you might feel a change in your personality, however there are changes you can make to assist you with adapting.

"This might be making another
job - like a craftsman, cook, or
volunteer, or
mastering another expertise.
Keeping your look on the
ongoing second instead of
The past can likewise truly assist
with feeling grounded. I
energetically suggest
contemplation or careful
exercises that take you back to
your body and the
Occasion."
 "Brain research brings a lot to
the table for individuals living
with memory issues,
whether this is support for family
members or the actual individual.
A consistent idea that winds
around itself through any
guidance with respect to
cognitive decline (whether you're
the one impacted or somebody
you love) is to
show restraint. Comprehend that
things might work diversely and
may take
additional time than previously.
Encircle yourself with help, get
proficient
exhortation, and realize that what
your identity is will continuously
run further than

memory.

CHAPTER III: HEALING AND RESILIENCE

BUILDING RESILIENCE

All in all, how would we beat trauma and fabricate our strength? Individuals frequently believe they're either conceived versatile and solid or powerless

and unfit to adapt. Yet, actually any of us can construct our versatility. It's an

expertise that we sustain and create.The other misinterpretation about

strength is that tough individuals generally feel better or cheerful. Flexibility

doesn't mean you generally feel better at the time or aren't impacted by

pressure. Part of turning out to be stronger to injury is figuring out how to
permit yourself to completely "feel" your feelings and go through the experience.In
the event that we return to considering trauma a trauma, in some cases we need to
permit wounds to ventilate and recuperate as opposed
to hold them under a wrap. We might have to apply a balm or treat wounds
with anti-infection agents. We can really focus on our bodies to develop our
fortitude and resistance. Getting appropriate rest, nourishment, and support
will permit us to recuperate quicker and all the more complete. Likewise, to
conquer an upsetting or horrendous experience, we should give ourselves an

opportunity to recuperate and use legitimate devices. A portion of these

instruments can emerge from inside (some are like the actions we would take

for actual wellbeing and recuperating). Different circumstances might expect

us to connect with a specialist or instructor for help. Steps on the way from

trauma to flexibility. These means include:

Checking out at the Involvement with another light

By reexamining our experience, we can get an alternate point of view

For instance, while working with a guide or specialist, they might have you

work out your experience, suppose it had happened to a companion, or talk it

through until it turns out to be less close to home and incorporating.Tracking down an Emotionally supportive network: A guide or specialists can offer

help during seasons of emergency. Companions, relatives, and care groups can likewise give a sounding board to examine sentiments and encounters.

Frequently connecting with another person can assist us with handling our

trauma.Recapturing a Feeling of Command over Our Lives. One truth about

tough individuals frequently feel they have command over their way ahead.

Thus, they frequently have an identity viability or the conviction that they can

successfully achieve their objectives and assume a functioning part in mending.

Dealing with Sense of pride: Self esteem or solid confidence is critical for pushing ahead, however it very well may be difficult to reestablish those

sensations of certainty when wrecked and harmed. One stage to resilience is

figuring out how to see the value in what our identity is and find our internal

assets.Reflecting and Getting the hang of: Building resilience is a growing

experience. We might need to investigate the past and acknowledge our job in

our conditions. We may likewise be adaptable and open to new methodologies

And thoughts for managing our stressors and issues.Working with an expert

psychological well-being instructor or specialist is perhaps the most remarkable

step you can take to construct flexibility. A specialist is somebody in your corner who can assist you with exploring through life's fights.

- **STRATEGIES FOR HEALING**

Frequently when we contemplate recuperating from trauma we ponder how overwhelming the excursion might be. We might try and decide to put off straightforwardly tending to our trauma on the grounds that the test might feel excessively perfect. Whether we decide to take part in the proper course of psychotherapy, there are numerous ways we can start to mend; techniques we can carry out procedures that might offer prompt help. While this rundown isn't thorough, it is an encouragement to ponder quick decisions we can make to decidedly impact the manner in which we see ourselves, our connections, and the world:

Get Support

The initial phase in making changes is to quit keeping quiet.

There is power in mysteries and when mysteries start to be opened, changes

can happen. Tell a confided in companion, a confided in relative, or a guide/specialist.

Recognize other people who can feel for your experience. There is solace in imparting our encounters and sentiments to other people

who "know". There are injury survivor bunches all around the nation and

many, run like 12-step recuperation programs, are for nothing. Numerous organizations in Chicago offer survivor gatherings, and Live Oak is the main

organization in Chicago — and in the Midwest, offering bunches explicitly

for gay male overcomers of life as a youngster of sexual maltreatment.

Deal with your body.

For the majority of us, injury includes some deficiency of command over our

bodies, so many of us who are survivors disengage from our bodies or don't
take great consideration of our bodies. Eating great, getting exercise, and
getting sufficient rest might sound excessively straightforward, however
These are three techniques that assist with making balance and a feeling of
establishing. Resting easier thinking about our body can likewise prompt
 better taking care of oneself in different regions.

Make something consistently.
A considerable lot of the lingering impacts of injury are put away in pieces
of the cerebrum that can't be gotten to through "talk". By participating in
imaginative and additionally expressive exercises, it is feasible to process (or
utilize) portions of the injury without talking about it. Drawing, painting,
photography, playing an instrument, and moving are only a few instances of

imaginative/expressive exercises that assist with handling injury and assist

getting us back in contact with the body.

Interface with nature.

One of the impacts of trauma can be a detachment with the world and the

bigger local area of living things. By reaching out with life's cycles, feeling a

more prominent association with others and the world in general is

conceivable. Place plants where they should be visible routinely. Go for

strolls by lakes, seas, mountains, valleys — whatever permits reconnection

with the bigger world. If conceivable, have a creature or pet as a component

of day to day existence. Really focusing on and getting unqualified love from

a creature can be a capably mending experience, and can be a forerunner to

Additional remunerating associations with others.

Interface with some power more prominent than oneself.

Trauma might leave us doubting the presence of God ("In the event that

there was a Divine being, the means by which could s/he let this happen to

me?"), so integrating some sort of otherworldly practice into day to day

existence is frequently useful. This needn't bother with being a coordinated

religion. It might very well be lighting a flame every day, discussing an

individual petition, making day to day customs, or interfacing with a more

coordinated, strict local area that offers help and mending.

Do relieving things.

Since trauma frequently makes us be in a consistent condition of caution as

well as seeing danger, taking part in exercises that lessen this more

a significant level of excitement can be hugely useful. Reflection, yoga,

Kendo, breathwork, knead, or different exercises that lower levels of excitement can help in feeling more grounded, more associated with the

body, and more associated with sentiments in a sensible manner.

Volunteer.

The demonstration of helping other people and feeling beneficial is a critical

counteractant to self-hatred, low confidence, and sensations of mediocrity

that much of the time is the consequence of injury. Tracking down ways of

finding reason by and by and to feel esteemed by others here and there

assists with making structure in our lives and gives an establishment from

which to reconstruct confidence.

Permit sentiments to be felt as they emerge.

Large numbers of us who have endured injury might have discovered that

feeling is frightening and when sentiments come up, they are to be pushed

down. On the off chance that we permit ourselves to feel the sentiments
really, we are more averse to participating in carrying on or damaging ways
of behaving to veil them. It might very well be useful to participate in
imaginative/expressive exercises when sentiments emerge with the goal that
they can be handled and delivered. In some cases keeping a diary is likewise
 useful as it permits sentiments and considerations to be recorded on paper
 and not put away in the head or body of the survivor.
 If conceivable, access a specialist or guide who is prepared in working with overcomers of trauma.
There are one of a kind issues that emerge for us as survivors and it's critical
that assuming treatment is a choice or decision, the advisor picked has
  extraordinary skill and aversion to these issues. Assuming fundamental, it's

vital to inquire as to whether the advisor picked has diminished rates or

debatable charges. Additionally, we ought not be reluctant to get some

information about unique preparation in working with the trauma(s) with

which we are managing. It's our entitlement to know the foundation,

experience, and the preparation of experts we welcome into our lives for help.

These ten procedures are not intended to act as a remedy for recuperating

from trauma, yet they are an encouragement to try different things with

mending now, securely, and right away. There might in all likelihood never

be   a "right" time to mend yet we can start mindfully, in little ways, everyday.

- **THERAPEUTIC APPROACHES**

While searching for a specialist, it is essential to remember that, paying little mind to what sort of psychotherapy you seek after, your specialist ought to

enable you and welcome you as a teammate in your treatment, not endeavor

to force command over you. Investigations have discovered that people who

are dynamic members in their treatment and are more happy with the

treatment. Likewise, it is essential that you have a good sense of reassurance

in your helpful relationship.

There is no supernatural treatment that will recuperate you short-term, nor is

there one type of psychotherapy that is ideal for everybody, except you ought

to have the option to track down a specialist, as well as a helpful

methodology, that works for you. Recuperating resembles a long distance race.

It requires readiness, rehashed practice, fortitude, assurance, and the help of

others — including that of an expert mentor or specialist.

While there are various treatment draws near, the reason for all trauma centered

treatment is to coordinate the awful accident into your life, not take away it.

This article talks about the most widely recognized types of trauma treatment.

Each approach is portrayed in its most unadulterated structure, yet remember

that numerous specialists join various sorts of treatments.

Pharmacotherapy

Pharmacotherapy is the utilization of drugs to oversee problematic trauma

responses. Prescriptions have been demonstrated to be useful with the

accompanying classes of responses/side effects:

Meddling side effects

Hyperarousal

Close to home reactivity

Increased excitement

Touchiness

Sorrow

Taking medicine doesn't make one's trauma responses and torment dissipate.

Meds can assist with making the side effects not so serious but rather more

reasonable.On the off chance that you choose to utilize meds, counsel a specialist

and keep working with that specialist however long you take the drugs. Educate

the specialist regarding what the drugs are meaning for you. A few prescriptions

have secondary effects that could conceivably be mediocre to you, and certain

individuals don't answer well to drugs. Drugs are best when people seek after

treatment simultaneously.

Conduct Treatment

The most widely recognized type of conduct treatment is openness. In

openness treatment, one steadily overcomes one's feelings of trepidation for

instance, the recollections of a horrendous mishap without the dreaded result

happening. Frequently, this openness brings about the singular discovering that the apprehension or pessimistic inclination is unjustifiable, which thusly permits the trepidation to diminish.

Openness treatment has been found to decrease tension and sorrow, work on friendly change, and coordinate the trauma memory. There are different types of openness treatment:

Imaginal openness: An individual envisions the dreaded occasion as clearly as could be expected.

In vivo openness: The openness happens in the treatment.

Efficient desensitization: The individual is presented to progressively more trepidation inciting circumstances. This openness is matched with unwinding.Openness treatment is a profoundly viable treatment for post traumatic stress (PTSD).

One more type of conduct treatment is Pressure Immunization Preparing (SIT),

otherwise called unwinding preparation. Stress Vaccination Preparing helps
people to oversee pressure and nervousness.

Mental Social Treatment

Mental social treatment (CBT) is grounded in the possibility that an
individual should address and change mistaken considerations and increment
information and abilities. Normal components of mental social treatment trauma
treatment include:
Showing people how to take to oversee nervousness and stress
Teaching people on typical responses to trauma
Openness treatment
Recognizing and assessing negative, mistaken, and unreasonable
considerations and supplanting them with additional exact and more positive
contemplations

EYE Development DESENSITIZATION AND Going back over (EMDR)

Advisors who perform EMDR
first get particular preparation
from an affiliation,
for example, the EMDR
Foundation or the EMDR
Worldwide Affiliation. An
EMDR meeting follows a preset
grouping of 8 stages, or stages.
Treatment affects
the individual in treatment
intellectually zeroing in on the
horrendous experience
or negative idea while outwardly
following a moving light or the
specialist's
moving finger. Hear-able tones
may likewise be utilized now and
again. Banter in
regards to whether eye
developments are genuinely vital
exists inside the area of
brain science, yet the treatment
has been demonstrated to be
exceptionally
compelling for the easing and
end of side effects of trauma and
other pain.

Hypnotherapy.
There is nobody directing head
for hypnotherapy. As a rule, a
trance specialist

directs the person in treatment
into an entrancing state, then
draws in the individual
in discussion or addresses the
individual about a specific
central question. Most
subliminal specialists trust that
the feelings and considerations
that a singular
comes into contact while under
entrancing are pivotal to
recuperating.

Psychodynamic Treatment
The objective of psychodynamic
injury treatment is to distinguish
which period of
the awful reaction till the
individual is caught in.
Whenever this is observed, the
specialist can figure out which
parts of the awful accident
obstruct the handling
and coordination of the injury.
Normal components of
psychodynamic treatment
include:
Considering the person's
formative history and youth
Setting accentuation grasping the
significance of the trauma
Taking a gander at what the
trauma has meant for the
singular's identity and

connections, as well as what has
been lost because of the
horrendous mishap

Bunch Treatment

There are a wide range of
gatherings for trauma survivors.
A few gatherings are
driven by specialists, others by
peers. Some are instructive, some
pay attention to
giving help, and different
gatherings are restorative in
nature. Bunches are best
when they happen
notwithstanding individual
treatment. A trauma survivor
should
pick a gathering that is in
accordance with where one is in
the recuperating
venture:
 Pick a gathering zeroed in on
taking care of oneself and
adapting abilities.

**Recalling and
grieving/survivor stage:** Pick a
gathering zeroed in on
recounting
the trauma story.

Reconnection/thriver stage:
Join a gathering that intends to
make association
with individuals.

Instructive gatherings are proper
during all stages.
Any advisor, paying little mind
to which sort of treatment she or
he works from,
wants to help you develop and
recuperate through your awful
experience.
Together, you and your specialist
will endeavor to recognize and
distinguish:
Where you are at in your
mending process.
Who you might want to be
what you might want to do when
you go into the
thriver stage
How you can arrive at that spot
from where you are presently.
Instructions to direct you through
this mending work.

CHAPTER IV: RECLAIMING YOUR HEALTH AND HAPPINESS

- **NURTURING PHYSICAL WELLBEING**

 Better Sleep

Studies have demonstrated that a lack of sleep can influence your mental

expression and abilities and could, in fact, prompt unfortunate eating habits. Difficulty dozing, absence of rest, and disturbed rest are normal side effects of numerous psychological well-being issues, including uneasiness and discouragement. Then again, when we are feeling intellectually well and have fewer distressing contemplations, our rest can further develop dramatically.

Identifying a mitigating rest routine can be a useful method for sustaining

sound propensities that uphold a casual state.

Increased Energy

At the point when we are encountering hardships with our psychological

well-being, including pressure, burnout, nervousness, or gloom, we frequently need

energy and might in fact
encounter serious exhaustion
subsequently.
Conversely, sustaining great
emotional wellness can prompt
inclination more
stimulated and certain about our
encounters, our current
circumstance, and the
connections in our lives.
Whether it's defining solid limits
for yourself, rehearsing Care or
investing time in
nature, focusing on taking care of
oneself can upgrade your energy
levels, work on
your rest, and move a
reestablished feeling of direction.
 Improved mood
While our state of mind can be
impacted in the event that we are
feeling disturbed
or focused, sustaining great
psychological well-being can
build sensations of joy
and energy. With less unpleasant
contemplations obfuscating our
psyches, we can
concentrate on the positive parts
of our lives.
One method for supporting our
emotional well-being is by
rehearsing cognizant

breathing activities.
This can assist us with noticing
our considerations and pay heed
to how we feel,
which thus assists us with
controlling our state of mind,
reflect, and introspect prior
to respond to any circumstance.
It likewise assists us with gaining
sound
propensities that empower us to
segregate from distressing
contemplations, realign
our aims, and support powerful
navigation.

- **CULTIVATING EMOTIONAL HEALTH**

In the rush of our day to day
routines, it's barely noticeable the
significant effect
close to home prosperity can
have on our general personal
satisfaction. In this blog,
we will dig into the idea of close
to home prosperity, investigating
what it means
and how it can prompt additional
enhancing connections and a
really satisfying
life.

Grasping Profound Prosperity

Close to home prosperity isn't
just about encountering bliss and
staying away from
bitterness. An all encompassing
methodology includes fathoming
and really
dealing with our feelings. It's tied
in with cultivating a profound
association with
our sentiments, communicating
them in useful ways, and creating
methodologies to
explore testing feelings.
Generally, it's the craft of
dominating our profound scene.
**The Force of The ability to
understand individuals on a
profound level -**
One of the vital apparatuses
chasing after close to home
prosperity is the capacity
to understand individuals on a
deeper level (EI). EI envelops
different features,
including mindfulness, self-
guideline, compassion, and
relational abilities. By
leveling up these abilities, you
can open the way to better
connections and a
seriously satisfying life.

Mindfulness: Understanding your own feelings is the most vital move towards
close to home prosperity. It's tied in with perceiving how you feel, why you feel as
such, and the effect these feelings have on your viewpoints and activities.
Mindfulness is the establishment whereupon the ability to appreciate anyone on a
profound level is constructed.

Self-Guideline: Whenever you've recognized your feelings, the following stage is
self-guideline. This includes dealing with your close to home reactions in a manner
that is solid and useful. It's the capacity to control rash responses and on second
thought answer nicely to circumstances.

Compassion: Sympathy is the extension that associates you with others on a
profound level. It's the ability to comprehend and discuss the thoughts of others.
By developing sympathy, you can extend your connections, encourage

understanding, and proposition backing to everyone around you.

Relational

Abilities: Compelling correspondence and relational abilities are vital

for profound prosperity. These abilities empower you to communicate your

feelings plainly, listen effectively, and explore clashes in a productive way.

- **BUILDING A FULFILLING LIFE**

Life is overflowing with promising and less encouraging times and here

And there it causes you to feel overwhelmed and in a not so great kind

of the way. It's huge for this circumstance that you return two or three

maneuvers toward contemplating your method of life

Get some much needed rest to Travel

You genuinely should rehearse balance between fun and serious activities to feel satisfied and cheerful. In any case, you risk encountering burnout and not playing out your best work

Consider your timetable right now and sort out when a great time is to

get some much needed rest to travel. Continue new experiences so you

can step outside your usual range of familiarity and have a great time.

Utilize your downtime to meet new individuals, attempt new food sources, and furthermore get some rest and unwinding so you can re-energize and

get back feeling prepared to return to your ordinary daily schedule.

Clean Up and Clean up Your Home

Your home life is one more fundamental piece of the riddle with regards to being cheerful and feeling satisfied. It's particularly significant and important assuming you telecommute. A muddled house can cause you to

feel more worried and you might
lose your things routinely for this
situation.
All things considered, get some
margin to clean and clean up
your spaces
regularly.
Go through your possessions and
dispose of or give what is not
generally required.
This will cause you to feel more
quiet when you are in your home
and you'll have
the option to find what you're
searching for all the more
rapidly.
You'll like investing energy at
home more frequently when it's
clean and liberated
from soil and wrecks.

**Encircle Yourself with Positive
Individuals**

Contemplate your group of
friends and about individuals you
are permitting
into your life and who you
cooperate with routinely. The
explanation is that
who you invest your energy with
additionally influences your
temperament
and life.

Accordingly, consider moving
away from people who are
pessimistic and put you
down. Put resources into
connections that are sound and
with individuals who have
your wellbeing on a basic level.
You'll feel a lot more joyful and
less restless when you decide to
encircle yourself
with good individuals.
Don't hesitate for even a moment
to fan out and meet new
individuals during the
time spent assessing your
different associations with
others.
When you have great
associations set up make sure to
connect and sustain these.
No one can really tell when you
will require somebody to listen
carefully or when
you simply need to get along
with somebody to enjoy a hearty
chuckle or cry.
Eat Right and Exercise
You should likewise accept great
consideration of yourself for the
best result
and practice taking care of
oneself. You can fabricate a
satisfying and

blissful life for yourself by treating your brain and body well. This involves eating a sound eating routine and getting a lot of activity. You'll rest better around evening time this way as well.

Start getting ready dinners for yourself at home so you have more command over the fixings and part estimates.

You may likewise need to keep a food diary to record what you're eating and distinguish any pain points.

Make certain to get a lot of work-out everyday regardless of whether it is fitting in additional means and strolling around your area.

Consider finding a responsible accomplice so both of you can keep each other roused to need to work out.

Self-Reflect and Ponder

In some cases everything necessary to lead a blissful and satisfying life is to set aside some margin to self-reflect. During the time spent self reflection,

you might have the option to track down answers for a portion of your
concerns. You might find a new and different way that you wish your life to
go during these minutes. Take a stab at moving a piece increasingly slow right now too. Rehearsing
care and contemplation will assist you with setting your considerations up and
you'll be more in contact with your sentiments.
Head off to someplace calm where you can unwind and be completely
submerged in the experience. Show restraint toward yourself on the grounds
that contemplating is generally difficult to at first do.
Start it and you'll before long notification every one of the advantages that
come from this kind of training. At the point when you are mirroring, it's likewise a decent chance to zero in on
your endowments and to be thankful for what you truly do have in your life.

This exercise can turn your mentality and demeanor around to improve things.

Get A new Line of work You Appreciate

Stirring takes up a considerable amount of your significant investment every

day. In this way, you ought to accomplish something you love and

appreciate. If not, it might feel like you're burning through your time and

abilities.In the event that you are in an impasse work at present, this may be

your opportunity to roll out an improvement. Consider and find what your

energy is and survey your assets to foster a decent vocation match for

yourself.

You need to ensure that you feel tested working and that your abilities are

 being put to utilize.

 If not, you might feel withdrawn and exhausted at your specific employment.

At the point when you love what you do, you'll awaken feeling roused to hold
 onto each new day and be more joyful generally speaking.
 Turn off from Innovation
 Looking at innovation and continuously being associated with your gadgets
 can negatively affect your wellbeing and prosperity and it can likewise be
 habit-forming.
 You should ensure that you enjoy reprieves to turn off from innovation to
 feel and be well. You'll probably find that you have all the more leisure time
 to partake in different exercises that don't include a screen.
 This way you can get a few new leisure activities or interests for yourself that
 you can do all things considered.
 Make an honest effort to downplay the time you're associated with for the best
 result.
 Contemplate investing more energy in nature rather than on your gadgets. Nature

can be extremely mending for yourself and this way you'll get all the more
 everyday advances and exercise.
 Turning off more frequently is great for your psychological well-being also.
 Accordingly, you'll feel more joyful and will actually want to utilize your leisure
 time and energy to pursue your life objectives.

Stay away from Examinations
You might observe that you're troubled right now since you're continuously
contrasting yourself with others. This can be impeding to your psychological
well-being and prosperity. All things considered, you ought to turn the
emphasis on you and attempt to be simply the most ideal form that you can
be.Fabricate a satisfying and cheerful life for yourself by focusing on the
objectives you set for you and investing less energy contrasting your
existence with others.

This is one more valid
justification to not generally be
associated via online
 entertainment since beginning
contrasting yourself with others
through these
sorts of outlets can be simple.
You can construct a satisfying
and blissful life for yourself by
utilizing your
 significant investment to deal
with yourself rather than
continuously thinking
often about the things others are
doing.

CONCLUSION

Troublesome occasions can make
a dependable negative difference.
Simply
recollecting that them would be
able raise pulse and deactivate
sane reasoning
pieces of a casualty's mind.
Large numbers of these
encounters came from youth
and have been around for a
longtime. Be that as it may, there
is potential for even

the nastiest of devils you
face.One procedure is pretty
much as straightforward as
getting a finger across a patient's
vision. As they follow the finger
with their eyes,
sound signs from the clinical
expert assistance,then make new
affiliations. EMDR
or eye development
desensitization and going back
over could sound insane, yet
it's ridiculously successful at
assisting individuals with
recuperating
from trauma. The explanation it's
so useful is a direct result of the
manner in which
it permits casualties to coordinate
their awful recollections. A
contributor to the
The issue with these occasions is
that their memory would be able
to work out as
though it's going on in the
present. Coordination takes into
consideration them to
Just add these occasions to a
memory bank as opposed to
naturally suspecting
they're genuine.Your body and
brain are surprisingly associated.
Sorting out how

your feelings work and effect your body is fundamental for equilibrium and
soundness in life.
Trauma makes this truly hard due to the manner in which it places a kind of
caution framework in our bodies. Individuals as a rule attempt to numb these sentiments with medication or liquor
misuse, or by exhausting themselves. However, these impermanent fixes just put a swathe on rather than concentrating on the real issues at hand. That is where
binding together the body and psyche with Yoga proves to be useful.
Yoga permits injury casualties a method for grasping feelings and how their body
handles them.
Care and an encouraging group of people of loved ones who care are too
extraordinary ways of encountering mending.
The point of care is to intellectually interface with and become mindful of your

body and feelings rather than
simply denying them. It's hard to
do this later
affliction since we could do
without to manage difficult
feelings like bitterness or
outrage. However, smothering
them, as numerous casualties do,
simply prompts
more issues. Exclusively by
standing up to your evil
presences might you at any
points start to recuperate from
them.
Contemplation procedures help
you reconnect with the manner in
which you truly
feel so that you can begin this
cycle.
This novel device can quiet the
effects of injury on the psyche
and body.
Whether it's downturn or
persistent torment, care can help.
It's additionally known
to fortify your insusceptible
framework, assist you with
controlling feelings, and
get your chemicals in better
equilibrium.
Connections are one more
imperative part of the
recuperation interaction. Your

organization of family,
companions, and clinical experts
can help you generally
have somebody to go to for help.
You can associate with other
supportive
Individuals through nearby AA
gatherings, strict gatherings, and
veterans'
associations.

0